STOKE-ON-TRENT PAST & PRESENT

KEVIN LONG

SUTTON PUBLISHING LIMITED

Sutton Publishing Limited
Phoenix Mill · Thrupp · Stroud
Gloucestershire · GL5 2BU

First published 2000

Copyright © Kevin Long, 2000

Title page photograph: Stoke Town Hall.

British Library Cataloguing in Publication Data
A catalogue record for this book is available from the
British Library.

ISBN 0-7509-2494-2

Typeset in 10.5/13.5 Photina.
Typesetting and origination by
Sutton Publishing Limited.
Printed in Great Britain by
Ebenezer Baylis, Worcester.

For Mum & Dad

CONTENTS

FOREWORD

As a newcomer to the ranks of local historians, Kevin Long has made an impressive debut and put to good use a selection of old photographs from the Potteries Museum collection. The start of a new millennium is obviously a good moment to look back into the past and see how much has changed in the Six Towns since the beginning of the twentieth century.

Every one of the 120-odd locations in the book was visited by the author, who took his own pictures. It's a familiar device to compare the past with the present, but Kevin has given it fresh appeal by choosing some subjects which are less than obvious. Pictures firmly in this category include the burnt-out ruins of the Greyhound pub at Penkhull in 1936, terraced houses in Bedford Street, Shelton, and bottle ovens in Williamson Street, Tunstall.

However, my own favourites are the pictures of Bratt and Dyke's lavishly decorated shopfront for a royal visit in 1924 and a procession of horse-drawn carriages across cobblestoned Albion Square, also in Hanley, in 1910 or thereabouts.

Kevin Long is clearly motivated by affection for his subject and has been at pains to get everything right. His book is a useful addition to Stoke-on-Trent's ever-growing library on local history.

John Abberley, 2000

ACKNOWLEDGEMENTS

Many thanks go to Alan Taylor for his help during this project, and to the Potteries Museum and Art Gallery, Stoke-on-Trent, for access to the photographic archive. Miss Greaves and Mr Elliott took many of the photographs used by permission of the museum; thanks go to them also. Thanks to the Staffordshire Schools History Service for permission to reproduce photographs. Thanks for photographic material, information and time also go to Norman Edwards, Julie Locker, Carol Ecclestone, John Abberley of the *Sentinel*, David Stockley of John Tams Group plc, Angela Lee of the Gladstone Pottery Museum, Yvette Hodgkinson of the *Sentinel*, Glen Parkes and Dave Foers. Although every effort has been made to ensure the information given in this book is correct, any errors are the author's responsibility.

INTRODUCTION

To write a book on the history of Stoke-on-Trent is a difficult task for even the most adept author. Locally, Ernest Warrillow (*A Sociological History of Stoke-on-Trent*) is probably the best-known character to achieve this. Over the years our city has changed dramatically, and it is difficult to imagine our mothers and grandmothers having to wait until the weekly industrial shutdown to be able to hang out their washing to dry. This was the case, however. The vast array of bottle kilns firing day and night would reduce any crisp white sheet into a literal negative of itself. It is also difficult to imagine a city creating its own insular atmosphere, and by this I do not refer to ambience.

To most people Stoke-on-Trent is 'The Potteries', was 'The Potteries', and always will be 'The Potteries'. However, my aim is to show that the City of Stoke-on-Trent is much more than just two words. From the images in this book you will see how the city as a whole has developed over the last century or so into what it is today.

Of course the city has not always been: it came about through the amalgamation of the six towns of Stoke, Hanley, Burslem, Tunstall, Longton and Fenton. As you will see these towns had identities all of their own; they were originally all small market towns and their layout was as such. They all had their own town halls, markets, parishes and even dialect, and it was debatable whether many people who lived in Burslem had ever been to Hanley and vice versa. Although the towns were close in proximity the local rivalry began at an early time, and before I go any further let me add that although we now have the City of Stoke-on-Trent we still have six very individual towns.

The six market towns were intertwined with small-scale industry, but with the coming of the industrial revolution natural development took place. Although markets were, and still are, a mainstay in the life of the towns, major developments in industries such as the 'pots' and the 'pits' took place, and redefined the area. In today's world industrial areas are sited well away from residential; however, in towns such as Hanley, Burslem and Longton of 200 years ago it was quite common to find a 'potbank' sited next to, if not within, a community housing area. In fact this was commonly due to the 'potbank' owner actually constructing the housing for his staff. After all, there is no excuse for being late to work if you live next door to the factory. It was around this time (late eighteenth century) that 'The Potteries' was born, and with it the rise of the coal industry. Add to this the growing iron and steel production, and this presented a thriving field of industry that took the area through the nineteenth and into the twentieth century.

Along with most industrial areas Stoke-on-Trent experienced major changes during the twentieth century. One of the first developments came in 1910 with the Federation Bill approved by Parliament: the six towns all came together under the banner of the County Borough of Stoke-on-Trent, and in 1925 King George V announced that it was to become a city. Other changes in the early part of the century included housing reform. With the increase in industry it was felt that the level of housing in the towns was inadequate, and it was decided in the early 1920s to extend the boundaries of the borough to create housing development away from the factories and mines. This led to areas such as Meir and Trent Vale seeing hundreds of council houses built within their confines. A postscript to this is that although on the face of it the working people would benefit by the new housing, this was not entirely the case. The rents for these new homes in idyllic surroundings proved too high for many workers, and they continued to live in the slum terraces of their township for the time being.

The twentieth century saw massive changes to the pottery industry with regard to technology, although it took a long time for these to be implemented because the workforce's methods had been handed down from generation to generation. This said, one improvement was implemented by Parliament. My comment in the opening paragraph is a fair reflection on the amount of smoke that was generated from the 'pots'; add to that the chimneys from the iron and steel works and you begin to realise what a polluted area Stoke was. In 1957 the Clean Air Act was passed by Parliament and this was the catalyst for a change in the atmosphere surrounding The Potteries. Over a period of time bottle kilns were replaced by gas and electricity driven kilns that reduced the pollution in the air by 95 per cent and allowed the people of Stoke-on-Trent to actually see their city for the first time.

Halfway through the century the mining industry of Stoke began to fall into decline. During the 1960s a major programme of pit closure ensued, rendering a once great industry almost helpless. The pain suffered by this industry does not stop there: during the 1980s the miners of North Staffordshire endured grave hardship owing to the strike of 1984–5, which became the longest national strike of the twentieth century. More pits closed in the 1990s, and 1998 saw the end of the mining industry in North Staffordshire with the closure of Silverdale Colliery. The same fate overtook the steel industry, when Shelton Bar closed in the 1970s. British Steel had planned the shutdown of the plant but after protests from the workforce, led by the late Ted Smith, it was reprieved. The plant was to stay open for a further two years, proving the protestors' argument that steel could be efficiently produced; however, after four months production ceased and the men were made redundant. In an interview some years later Ted Smith said 'it ripped the heart out of the City . . .'. He was probably right.

It was not all doom and gloom during the 1970s, however. At this time the City Council embarked on massive land reclamation schemes. The city was littered with slagheaps from the mines and marl holes from the pots. This presented a unique opportunity: put the heap into the hole. Although it was not as easy as it appeared this was precisely what the City Council decided to do; a fine example is the Berryhill project of 1971 which gave the city 70 acres of industrial and residential land. Another fine reclamation project brought us Central Forest Park in Hanley, for which the council should be congratulated. It is difficult to believe that the park was once nothing more than a slagheap. In fact the National Garden Festival of 1986 was located on land reclaimed from Shelton Bar. More changes for the better came for transport and communications with the building of the A500, known locally as the D-road, in the early 1970s. This project created a link with the M6 motorway for all the towns. The road development was added to in the 1990s with the new A50 dual carriageway running from the A500 through to the M1 at Nottingham. There are, of course, many other developments too numerous to mention, but you will see many in the illustrations of this book.

Although this introduction has only covered a small part of the history of Stoke-on-Trent, it has touched on some changes for the better and some for the worse. Although it is good to reminisce it is also important to realise that not all change and development is detrimental. Through this book you will see the changes that have taken place at various locations, and to buildings, industry and leisure facilities; you will see the good with the bad and the past with the present. The compiling of this book has been a labour of love and has taken me on a fascinating journey through history; it has also given me the opportunity to appreciate what we have today.

Kevin Long, 2000

CHAPTER ONE

STOKE

Aerial view of Stoke, *c.* 1933.

The Free Library and School of Art on London Road, Stoke, was opened in 1878 and was originally designed to hold the museum collections of the Potteries Athenaeum. This magnificent example of Gothic architecture was designed by Charles Lynam in 1877. The three separate sections at the front are covered in coloured tile mosaics, and the image of William Shakespeare adorns the middle one. This photograph was taken in May 1975.

The library has not changed that much in the twenty-five years that separate these two pictures. In fact it has hardly changed in the last 100 years, the only notable change being the process of age.

The Minton Memorial Building, also on London Road, May 1975. It was built in 1858 and originally housed the School of Art and Science. In 1861 public baths were added to the rear of the building.

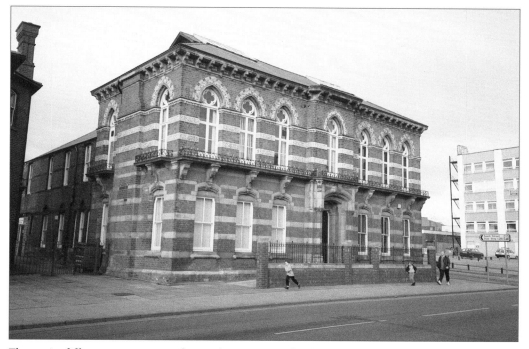

The main difference apparent today is the access to the front entrance. It is ironic that the first picture should show a vehicle for the disabled parked outside the building, yet no apparent entrance. Today a ramp has been built specifically for the disabled.

Employees from Minton's earthenware factory on their lunch break, *c.* 1910. Notice how imposing the factories of this day were; add to that the black colouring from the pot firings and you are confronted with an intimidating view.

The scene here today is very different, as the Minton's factory has been demolished and replaced by a car park. The claustrophobic feeling of this part of the town has also been removed.

We are now looking towards Campbell Place from London Road, late 1950s. At the top of the road can be seen the old Wheatsheaf public house, originally a coaching inn. At the centre of Campbell Place stood, for many years, a statue of Colin Minton Campbell who was a Member of Parliament for Stoke from 1880 to 1883. The statue was moved in 1954 and now stands outside Minton House on London Road. To the right is the walkway alongside the old Newcastle Canal, which ran right under this scene. The tall chimney in the background belonged to pottery manufacturers Spode Ltd.

Campbell Place still has the Wheatsheaf pub; however, the building was replaced in the 1960s. The row of shops on the right of the picture has doubled in size, which has been possible because of the reclamation of the canal. The only physical reference linking the two photographs is the Spode chimney.

Judging by the prominent shadows, this image of Church Street was taken on a bright, sunny day, c. 1910. In the centre of the street is an electric tram on its way to Fenton. The building on the right, occupied by Riseley's grocery, was probably the only white building in Stoke at that time.

It seems astonishing that the buildings on both sides of this main thoroughfare should remain unchanged for almost a century, but this is what we see in Church Street today. If we could ignore the buses and modern road markings it would be easy to forget the date of this photograph.

The Hippodrome Picture House in Kingsway, *c.* 1920. The detail in this photograph is fascinating; notice how everyone in the queue is sporting headwear of some description. It is also notable that all eyes are fixed on the photographer – as cameras were not all that common in the early 1920s.

The Hippodrome went on to become the Gaumont but was closed in 1961 and replaced by a simplistic row of retail units. Owing to a change in lifestyles a magnificent theatre has been sacrificed for modern luxuries such as a balti house, all night café and hairdressers.

Old slum cottages in Vinebank Street, previously known as Vine Street, October 1960. The industrial chimney in the background was the property of Elton Pottery.

The chimney is no more, and neither are the cottages: modern bungalows have replaced them.

The Greyhound public house in Penkhull, 1936. Penkhull is one of the earliest recorded settlements in the area, probably because there was good visibility from this elevated position. The Greyhound is significant as it used to be the courthouse for Newcastle-under-Lyme. It was partially destroyed by fire in 1936; this photograph was taken before rebuilding ensued.

After the fire the Greyhound was rebuilt to its former glory and, apart from the internal timber frame and front wall, remains unchanged to this day. Today it boasts 'Hot and Cold Food' and 'Quality Ales and Lagers'. Cheers.

The North Stafford Hotel, which has stood in Minton Square opposite Stoke railway station since 1848, photographed in the nineteenth century. In the foreground is a statue of the master potter and prominent businessman Josiah Wedgwood. Notice the horse-drawn carriage at the foot of the picture; it was probably waiting to take railway passengers to their final destination.

The cars and the trees make up the differences in these images. The North Staffs Hotel, seen here in early 2000, is still a fine sight to greet any traveller arriving in The Potteries by rail for the first time.

The Falcon Goss works in Sturgess Street, May 1975. Falcon Pottery was established after William Henry Goss left Spode in 1858 to pursue his own venture.

Portmeirion Pottery, named after the famous Gothic-style village in North Wales, acquired this site, then known as Gray's Pottery, in 1961. In 1986 Portmeirion built a new three-storey factory fronting on to London Road; the buildings we see here are no longer in use.

The bottle oven of the potters' miller W.J. Dolby, of Lytton Street. The calcinating of flint and fritt for use in the pottery industry took place here. Work ceased at this site in 1967.

Although it is one of the few bottle ovens to avoid demolition no attempt has been made to preserve it. However, it is in remarkably good condition and looks much as it did the day production stopped.

The frontage of the Minton Hollins building, Shelton Old Road, May 1975. This part of the factory, also the main entrance, was designed by Charles Lynam; built in 1868, it was used for warehousing and offices. The last section of the factory left standing, it finally closed in 1987.

Caudwell Communications & Technology Ltd saved the magnificent Minton Hollins building in 1992 and with the help of a grant restored it throughout. Caudwells are the UK's leading mobile phone distributor; a modern industry has now embraced Stoke-on-Trent.

Utilising Italian influences, Robert Scrivener designed the Cliffe Vale Pottery, Shelton New Road, for Thomas Twyford in 1887. Twyford used this factory for his sanitary ware and the factory is perfectly situated, only yards from road, rail and canal.

Caradon Twyfords moved to Kidsgrove, on the periphery of the city, in the early 1980s and left a once thriving factory to fall into disrepair. The frontage, seen here, is all that is left. There are plans to convert this impressive structure into offices; development started in 1999.

A much earlier scene showing the full scale of Thomas Twyford's factory. Note the horse and cart convoy at the entrance to the works.

Although the factory has long been demolished the frontage still stands proud along Shelton New Road.

On the face of it, this is quite an ordinary shop, photographed in January 1973. However, this building was originally a tollhouse when the road from Stoke to Hanley was turnpiked in the eighteenth century.

Still in use as a shop today, this newsagent's is actually called Tollgate News. As the advertisement suggests, why not 'call here for your *Sentinel*'?

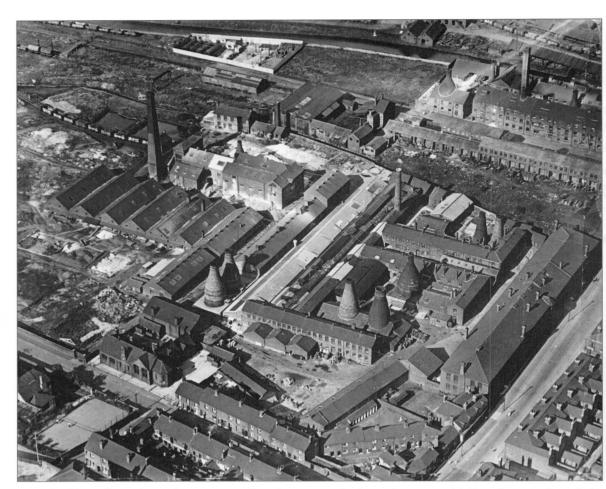

A 'potbank' in all its glory. The Minton Hollins factory was built on this site in 1868 and survived until the 1980s. This view clearly shows the mill, slip houses and preparation areas at the rear, then on to the tile making workshops, through the bottle ovens and into the packing house at the front. It was purpose built for mass tile production, with the concentration on efficiency.

CHAPTER TWO

HANLEY, ETRURIA & SHELTON

An aerial view of Hanley, late 1950s.

Hanley Market Square with the market in full swing, *c.* 1905. The two buildings shown are the old Market Hall, with the entrance to the market at the centre, and the Angel Hotel. The Market Hall was opened in 1849 on the site of the former Swan Inn. Most of the Angel disappeared in the early 1970s, and the Market Hall was demolished in 1981 to clear the way for the Potteries Shopping Centre.

Market Square is an entirely different scene today. The market has relocated to Fountain Square and the only common factor between the images is a portion of the Angel Hotel, which was left standing after most of it was demolished. Abbey National now operates from these premises.

Another view of Market Square showing the market sellers peddling their wares directly from their wagons, early 1900s. Was this Hanley's first ever car boot sale?

It would now be impossible for the market wagons of yesteryear to reach their original pitch, owing to the pedestrianisation of the area.

Lamb Street, 1940s. Huntbach's department store was established in the 1860s by Michael Huntbach. In 1977 Littlewoods acquired the building and proceeded to demolish it to make way for a new store.

The Littlewoods store that was opened in 1978 and cost over £3 million to build. Closer inspection of Lamb Street shows that all but one of the buildings that were present in the 1940s have disappeared; the one to remain unfortunately looks out of place amongst the modern frontages.

An unusually quiet scene at Crown Bank, Hanley, 1920s. In the centre of the picture is the Crown Bank Hotel alongside Millers House Furnishing, later to become George Mason's grocery shop. Just outside the hotel was a common feature of the area at this time – underground toilets!

Banking institutions now dominate the scene around Crown Bank. The building that housed the Crown Bank Hotel has now become the Midland Bank and the Trustee Savings Bank has succeeded the Marquis of Granby. The toilets have been moved upstairs.

The building we see here was erected in
1933 on Stafford Street for McIlroy's
department store. It was purchased by
Lewis's in 1935 and demolished in 1964
when the store moved to new purpose-built
premises further along Stafford Street.

Following the demolition of the old Lewis's in 1964 the site was used to build a series of small retail
units with offices above. However, owing to the success of the Potteries Shopping Centre, many of
these units today lie empty.

Piccadilly, Hanley, early 1970s. Note Radio Stoke in the background.

Most of the commercial development in Hanley has been in the vicinity of the Potteries Shopping Centre, and the scene around Piccadilly has barely changed.

Oliver Bratt and Henry Dyke opened their Trinity Street store in 1896 some twenty years after forming their partnership. The store was built on the site of the old Roebuck Inn. Here the store is shown decked out for the visit of the Prince of Wales in 1924. Unfortunately the doors closed for the last time in 1989.

The building today looks quite different with the central pediment removed and the addition of a fourth storey. A large proportion of the ground floor has been taken over by HFC Bank, whilst the upper storeys are occupied by a number of businesses.

McIlroy's department store, Miles Bank, Hanley. McIlroy's took over from Boulton and Thomas in 1883: they built a good reputation as the 'people providers' and specialised in everything. They sold out to Lewis's in 1935, and the building shown here was demolished in 1964.

The building that now stands on this site is made up of retail units and offices. One retailer, Another World, offers 'Sci-Fi, Fantasy, Horror, Cult Film & TV, Collectables, American Pop Culture, The Weird and Bizarre'. It is unquestionably another world.

This photograph was taken from Lamb Street and shows the top of Market Square and the beginning of Parliament Row on High Street (now Town Road). At the top of the picture is the Manchester and Liverpool District Bank sited next to Boots, the chemist. It would be a long time before this area would be pedestrianised.

On Parliament Row today NatWest (who acquired the Manchester and Liverpool District Bank) and Boots can be found cohabiting. Further down the Row we can see Woolworth's and Marks & Spencer. The building on the right of the picture has since had its roof levelled and is now occupied by the jewellers H. Samuel.

The Old Town Hall of Hanley, built in 1845 on the site of a former butter market in Fountain Square. In 1886, when the Borough moved its base to what had been the Queen's Hotel in Albion Street, Lloyds Bank purchased the Hall. The old building survived until its demolition in 1936.

The current building central to this scene was built by Lloyds Bank in 1936, and now carries the name Lloyds TSB following the merger of the two banks. The Woolwich Building Society occupies the building to the left of the picture; this building dates back to the late nineteenth century and has previously housed the Leeds and Halifax building societies.

The current Town Hall, Hanley, designed by R. Scrivener & Sons. The Queen's Hotel in Albion Street had been built in 1869. In 1887–8 the Victoria Hall was added at the rear to a design by the borough surveyor Joseph Lobley.

The Town Hall has hardly changed at all and is still in use today.

The Grand Theatre of Varieties was built on the corner of Trinity Street and Foundry Street and opened in 1898. It was converted into a cinema in 1931 but some months later was gutted by fire. It stood abandoned until its replacement was built in 1936: the fire had caused widespread damage, and it was decided to build a new cinema, the Odeon, on the site. The new building was opened in 1937 and was very successful, but with the advent of television audiences dwindled during the late 1960s, and the doors of the Odeon closed in November 1975.

In the 1990s this purpose-built cinema was completely gutted and refurbished as a trendy café bar. True to its theatrical tradition it was christened The Foyer.

The Regent opened in Piccadilly in 1929; it was the first cinema in the area to show a talking picture. In the 1950s the Regent changed names to become the Gaumont and changed again in 1975 to become the Odeon. The cinema saw some development work in the mid-1980s but closed towards the end of 1989, when the new Odeon opened at Festival Park.

With the advancement of the 'Cultural Quarter' in Hanley the time was right to reopen the building as a theatre, and this happened in the summer of 1999. The Regent has so far been very successful, ending 1999 with the pantomime *Cinderella*, starring Melinda Messenger and Britt Ekland.

This snowy scene shows the Theatre Royal during rebuilding work, which took place after a fire had destroyed it in 1949. The theatre reopened in 1951 with *Annie Get Your Gun*, but was to close some ten years later. The Theatre Royal Restoration Trust reopened the theatre, fully restored, in the early 1980s.

Here we see the same scene today. Although the theatre has gone through troubled times during the 1990s it has managed to stay open, and still stages excellent productions.

Another view of Crown Bank, this time looking up from Piccadilly. Two groups of men are standing outside the Crown Bank Hotel: licensing laws in those days were fairly strict and it appears they have arrived just too early. Notice the advertisement for Parkers Ale above the Marquis of Granby; it was a popular brew in Hanley during the early part of the twentieth century.

It is notable that in the Crown Bank scene of today there are no chimneys. Before the advent of central heating it would have been necessary to have a coal fire in every room, hence the number of chimneys in the previous image. The four chimneys on the roof of the Crown Bank Hotel indicate that it may have had as many as twelve coal fires to keep the patrons from catching a chill.

There are many things in this image of Albion Square, *c.* 1910, that would be out of place in today's world – the cobbled streets, the tramlines, the horse and carriage procession and the boaters to name just a few. One thing that does not change: the streets are lined for a procession of any variety.

Albion Square looks very different today. On the corner now stands Tigers pub in a very fine building; in the centre of Old Hall Street there is a floral display sponsored by the City Council, C & A and Wilkinson's.

Etruria Vale Road looking towards Shelton Bar, May 1960. In the centre of the picture is the Duke of Bridgewater public house. There are factory chimneys on the skyline, and to the extreme right is a slagheap created by Hanley Deep Pit.

Two changes that greatly affected the city are depicted in this image. The disappearance of the many chimneys of Shelton Bar, with the closure of the plant in the 1970s, is a major development in the history of the area. The aforementioned slagheap has been reclaimed to give us part of the Festival Park retail scheme.

Looking towards Brunswick Street we can see that the Theatre Royal is in the process of being rebuilt after the fire, 1950. It only took the fire just over an hour to do enough damage to cause the collapse of the roof. Because the Government refused to grant a licence, rebuilding took nearly two years.

The building to the left of the picture was for many years an Army and Navy-type store; it is now an excellent Italian restaurant called Portofino. The theatre still stands in the centre of the picture, but the small row of shops has been replaced by a retail and office block.

Bedford Street, Shelton, October 1960. This row of old terraced housing is situated across from the Ridgeway pottery. Note the old ceramic boot-cleaning device at the foot of the door. These houses were black with smoke from the firing of the Ridgeway bottle ovens only 50 yards away.

The houses were cleared during the late 1960s. The probable reason was their proximity to the factory and the poor conditions that this brought. The area now adds to the greenery of the city and is quite close to the Caldon Canal walkway.

Jesse Shirley built the Etruscan Bone & Flint Mill to a George Kirk design in 1857; Kirk was a local builder who specialised in mills. It was used to grind flint and bone for the pottery industry. The steam engine that drove the mill was called the 'Princess' and was built in the 1830s in Lancashire. The mill ceased production in 1972.

The Etruscan Mill, which has been classified as an ancient monument since 1975, is now the focal point of the Etruria Industrial Museum, and the last steam-powered bone and flint mill in Europe. On the first weekend of every month the 'Princess' can be seen in steam.

The Round House is the only surviving structure of Josiah Wedgwood's works in Etruria. Once part of a pair its exact function is not known; however, it is thought that at some time it may have served as storage or offices. This photograph was taken in the early 1960s just after the demolition of the Wedgwood factory.

The *Sentinel* offices now occupy this site and the Round House stands in the corner of the car park. The *Sentinel* opened here in 1987 and it was decided to restore the Round House as a feature. It currently houses an old printing press and is part of the *Sentinel* guided tour.

This intricately designed building is the old Telephone Exchange at the junction of Marsh Street and Clough Street, Hanley, July 1974. Built in 1888, it was in use until the early 1970s. The aesthetic beauty of this particular building has always been in question: to the people of Hanley it is one of those things you either love or hate.

At the time of going to press the old Telephone Buildings were in the throes of conversion, and are due to open sometime during 2000 as the Telephone Exchange public house.

Thomas Hinde built Smithfield Pottery on Lower Mollart Street in 1880. It was leased to Robert Sherwin in 1929 and closed in 1984. It was destined for demolition to make way for the new Hanley ring road but was reprieved; it is now a Grade II listed building. This photograph was taken in September 1980. The tall building in the background is Utility House, which was used by the City Council until the late 1990s; it is now empty.

Shortly after being renovated the old potbank was reopened as Donovan's Wine Bar, and in 1993 it was transformed into a restaurant; 1999 saw another reincarnation, this time as Bourbon Street Jazz Bar & Restaurant. Shortly after this photograph was taken in early 2000 the For Sale sign was put up again. Let's hope this little piece of Stoke-on-Trent history gets yet another new lease of life.

The diggers move in to demolish the Shelton Bar. In the distance is Etruria Hall. Since the 1860s the growing steel works had encroached on to the grounds of the Hall, eventually swallowing up the building itself, when it was used as offices. Here we see the clearing of the land that would be reclaimed as the site of the National Garden Festival which took place in 1986.

After the National Garden Festival a number of developments took place on this site, which is now called Festival Retail Park. The park has attracted many businesses, such as Morrison's supermarket, B&Q DIY and Toys R Us, all of which have large retail units. The park has also attracted many office-based businesses, such as KPMG Accountants. This shot was taken from what is now the local water park, Water World.

The Charles Street Wesleyan chapel was built in 1819 and here a mass of people arrive for a service, *c.* 1898. The chapel could hold nearly 800 people and regularly drew over 500 during the early part of the nineteenth century.

On the site today we have the Hanley Shopping Centre, not to be confused with the much larger Potteries Shopping Centre. The centre backs on to the Hanley bus station and includes numerous shops, Argos and Wilkinson's to name but two.

The Empire Picture House in Trinity Street, Hanley. This theatre had an inventive design: it was a tall white building with two stone pillars, one either side of the entrance, and also had a domed canopy above. The cinema closed and was later demolished in 1956.

The same scene today shows us that the site of the Empire is now the home of a shopping arcade, which leads through to Piccadilly.

Thomas Mawson designed Hanley Park, including Cauldon Gardens, which is seen here in about 1905. Cauldon Gardens was completed in 1894 and Alderman E.J. Hammersley donated the fountain in the same year. In the background we can see the conservatory, built in 1893.

The actual layout of Cauldon Gardens has not changed and the fountain still stands, but the conservatory was demolished in 1986. Each of the six towns benefited from their own parks with the exception of Stoke, owing to the close proximity of Hanley Park.

This view of Pall Mall in 1930 shows the old museum, the Mechanics' Institute and the British Workman public house. The Mechanics' Institute was built in 1861 and went on to house the public library. The museum was extended in 1927 to include an art gallery, and after the move to the new museum in 1956 the upper storey of the building was taken down, having become unsafe. Eventually all but the pub were demolished.

Sitting alone at the top of Pall Mall is the British Workman. No longer a pub, it has been closed for some years; however, it did make a short-lived reappearance as a hair salon. The massive structure to the left of the picture is the redeveloped Regent Theatre, which opened its doors to the public again in 1999.

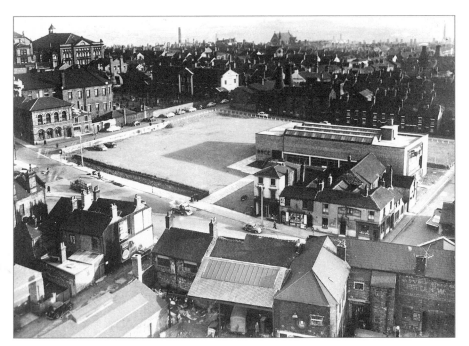

Costing £46,000, the new museum opened in 1956. It was built on part of the former site of Bell Pottery. Across from the site is the Bethesda chapel, dubbed the 'Cathedral of the Potteries' until its closure in 1985. In the 1980s the museum underwent major development, and now covers the whole site seen here.

The museum is now four times the size of the original structure built on this site. Above the entrance is a fine brickwork frieze depicting the various stages of pottery manufacture. The museum has an excellent collection including examples of pottery from all the leading manufacturers, some stretching back over 200 years, and also boasts a Spitfire fighter plane. The plane stands in honour of Reginald Mitchell, who designed it and many other aeroplanes. Mr Mitchell was born in the area and is regarded as one of Stoke's famous sons.

Trinity Street, Hanley, *c.* 1914. A confident boast from Theo Hughes states that he is an 'Authorised Plumbing Contractor for all kinds of Property Repairs'. The signwriter next door obviously helped with the advertising and so he should; Theo also owned that business.

All the buildings in the image above were demolished in the 1920s and replaced with the magnificent *Sentinel* offices, which opened in 1930. The *Sentinel* were to occupy this building until their move to the site of the old Wedgwood factory in 1987. This building, now known as Midland House, unfortunately stands empty.

Here we see a current image, 4 January 2000, of the First World War memorial situated outside the Town Hall, Hanley. The memorial dates from about 1920 and consists of an ashlar pedestal supporting the figure of a triumphant saint, cast in bronze. A grade II listed building, the memorial has the message 'They died for our freedom' inscribed on the rear of the pedestal. The memorial now also commemorates the fallen of the Second World War.

CHAPTER THREE

BURSLEM, COBRIDGE & MIDDLEPORT

Part of the Royal Doulton Works, Nile Street, Burslem, February 1974.

Looking towards the old Town Hall of Burslem from Newcastle Street. Architect G.T. Robinson designed the old Town Hall, with its classical façade, and it was opened in 1857. It ceased to be used as a town hall in 1911 and has had various uses since, two of which were the library in the 1960s and a leisure centre in the 1980s.

The view today is very much the same. The shops' owners have changed and there are no canopies.

Another view of the old Town Hall. Burslem, is decorated for the royal visit of 1924. In the background is the 'Shambles' meat market; built in 1836, it was demolished in the late 1950s.

All the shops to the left of the picture have been replaced with modern, plain-fronted buildings and the celebrations have long passed. There is a notable gap behind the old Town Hall; the 'Shambles' is gone but not forgotten.

The Big House, Swan Bank, February 1974. This house was originally built in 1751 as a dwelling for Thomas and John Wedgwood. The story of this house became intertwined with the Chartist movement, the uprising of the poorly paid masses against their oppressors, of the mid-nineteenth century. During the riots of 1842 Joseph Heapy, a protestor, was shot dead by the militia. Justifiably so, said the authorities.

Its address officially 1 Moorland Road, The Big House was occupied for many years by the Midland Bank. It now stands empty awaiting new occupants for the new millennium.

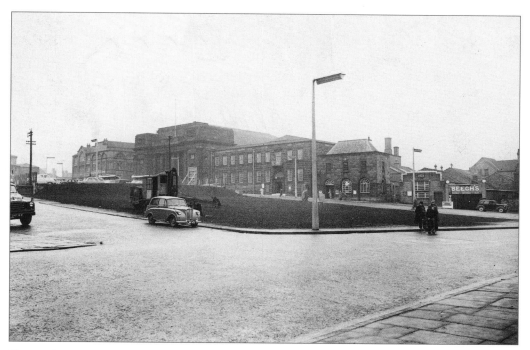

This is the site on which stood the 'Shambles' meat market until its demolition in 1958. This building was a favourite of Arnold Bennett's and featured in some of his novels. In the background are the Queens Theatre and the post office.

In 2000 a new pottery and art exhibition centre will open on the old 'Shambles' site. Construction was in progress as this photograph was taken.

The Wedgwood Institute in Queens Road, seen here during the Second World War, was opened in 1869. A great proportion of the frontage is decorated with mosaic tiles that depict the months of the year and the signs of the Zodiac. It was designed by R. Edgar and J.L. Laping, and has served a number of functions. The library was here for a while.

The Institute still houses Burslem Library today. A project to pedestrianise this area was underway when this picture was taken, and Queen Street was closed – hence the lack of activity.

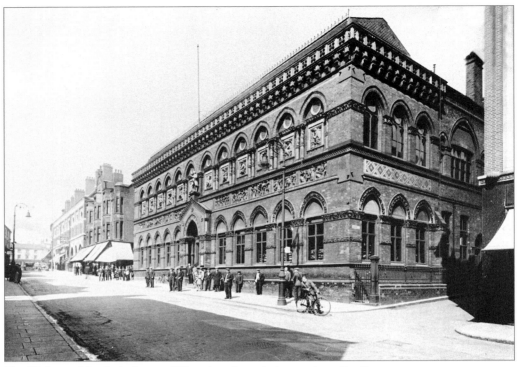

The Wedgwood Institute from a different angle and at a much earlier time.

The style of the street lamps has changed, but not much else.

A view of Fountain Square looking across to Westport Road (formerly Liverpool Road), 1904. The building just behind the fountain is the only remaining section of Enoch Wood's Fountain Place Works, which had been built on the site in 1789. To the left of the picture is the Manchester and Liverpool District Bank.

NatWest now occupies the building to the left of the picture and what remains of the Fountain Place Works is currently being converted into sixteen luxury apartments. A fountain still stands in the square, although not the original.

The fountain. Fountain Square, Burslem. This, the original fountain, was given by Enoch Wood for use by the public.

Although almost identical, the new fountain has only been standing here since 1990.

Fountain Square, *c.* 1905. Here we can see Nicklin's Drapery, Sandbach Drapery and The Cash Clothing Company, as we look towards Queens Street.

Although the names have changed the buildings remain the same, and work continues to pedestrianise the Square.

A favourite meeting place in Burslem at the turn of the century was St John's Square. Note the groups of people just standing around chatting. The Square also harboured some shops; on the opposite side is Lovatt's outfitters and tailors, whilst on the right there stand three public houses – the Masons, the Duke and the Bull's Head.

There isn't much in the way of change in St John's Square today. The centre of the Square has been used as a car park for a few years, but this may change with the increase of pedestrian areas in the heart of Burslem.

Port Vale playing at their new ground, Vale Park, in the 1960s. It was planned to become the 'Wembley of the North'; however this never materialised. Port Vale have been recognised as the second team of the Potteries because of the past successes of Stoke City; however, it was 'The Vale', as they are affectionately known, who played their home matches a stone's throw from the city centre. During the mid-1960s the manager of 'The Vale' was none other than the 'Wizard of Dribble', the late, great Sir Stanley Matthews. Sadly Sir Stan passed away on 23 February 2000, and will be dearly missed by all in the area. He was undoubtedly the greatest footballer of them all.

Many improvements have taken place at Vale Park since 1950: new stands have been built and the ground is now all seating. The team have performed well, currently in the Nationwide First Division. They lifted the Autoglass Trophy in 1993 and include Robbie Williams amongst their celebrity fan base.

Looking almost identical to Enoch Wood's factory (p. 69) is John and Richard Riley's Hill Top works, built in 1814. The building shows the Wade Heath name, dating this picture to the 1950s.

Although the building has been adapted over the years it is still possible to identify the arched coaching entrance and the stone dressed window. It now bears the name Wade.

Yet another scene of Royal celebrations in Burslem: Royal Doulton in Nile Street is preparing to receive a blue-blooded visitor. Henry, the son of founder John Doulton, moved to these premises through buying shares in an established pottery firm. The building to the extreme left is Holy Trinity Church, built in 1852. Owing to mining subsidence it was deemed unsafe, and was demolished in 1959.

Today the headquarters of Royal Doulton have moved to Minton House in Stoke after relocation during the 1970s; in Nile Street are the visitors' centre and museum. This is one of the largest of the pottery groups and includes Royal Crown Derby and Royal Albert.

The Moorcroft works at Sandbach Road, Cobridge, looking towards Burslem, October 1974. William Moorcroft built this factory after forming his own company in 1913. In stark contrast to other pottery works this is a single-storey structure and originally had three bottle ovens. The factory was not sited by canal or railway, and horse and cart transported all raw materials and finished ware.

W. Moorcroft plc still operate, from the original factory on Sandbach Road, but the Moorcroft family no longer own the business. Although no longer in use, one of the bottle ovens has been preserved. It was opened to the public on 25 November 1971.

Owned by Burgess and Leigh, manufacturers of Burleighware, Middleport Pottery was built in 1888 and described as 'the model pottery of Staffordshire'. This is the main entrance. The works was also single-handedly responsible for the rise of Middleport as a residential area.

Walking through the gates of this factory is akin to walking directly into the past. Many of the original buildings, including a bottle oven, have been retained. Burgess & Leigh Ltd owned the company until it went into receivership in June 1999; the current owners are Burgess, Dorling & Leigh Ltd.

In the graveyard of St John's Church is the resting place of Molly Leigh, who was believed locally to be a witch. It is said that after the funeral she was seen at her cottage. Through fear the townsfolk exhumed her body and repositioned the grave to face west (at right angles to the others). She was never seen again. This photograph was taken in 1974.

The Norman tower of St John's Church still stands proudly overlooking a graveyard that has seen much improvement over the last decade. Many graves had been desecrated, but now the grass has been cut and the stones repaired, and the bottle ovens of Acme Marls are as much neighbours now as they were when built in the 1930s.

Many people are gathered around Burslem war memorial in 1924. In the bottom right of the picture you can see the bonnet of the car carrying the Prince of Wales, who was visiting the town.

Public access to the First World War memorial is not what it was, but the continuing pedestrianisation of Burslem will help.

Here we see the old Swan Bank Methodist chapel. Built in 1801 and enlarged in 1816 to seat 1,290 people, it was an intimidating sight. The chapel's façade was remodelled in the 1870s.

The old Swan Bank Methodist chapel was replaced with the modern building seen here to the left of the picture in 1971. It is felt by many locals that the eerie presence of the chapel remains. The central building in this scene is the George Hotel, which was rebuilt on its original site in 1929.

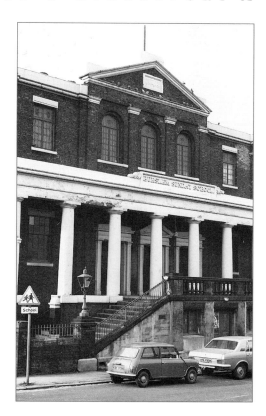

The Hill Top chapel, Westport Road, February 1974. The chapel was built in 1836 and was the head of the Burslem Methodist circuit. Built to a classical design, it was fronted with a spectacular portico.

The chapel was closed in 1977, and a fire some years later caused terminal damage. The main building was demolished in 1987, and today only the portico remains.

The Overhouse Manufactory, Wedgwood Place, Burslem, February 1974. The stone inscription above the main entrance reads: 'Edward Challinor commenced business here in AD 1819 and rebuilt the premises AD 1869'.

Barratts of Staffordshire now occupies the Overhouse Pottery building.

Brick House Street from Queen's Street looking towards Market Place, Burslem. Rising above the skyline is the top of the Old Town Hall. In this area poultry was killed before being taken to market.

It is quite remarkable, in a town where all main areas are virtually unchanged, that a small street such as this should see every structure replaced within the space of fifty years – all but the Wedgwood Institute of course.

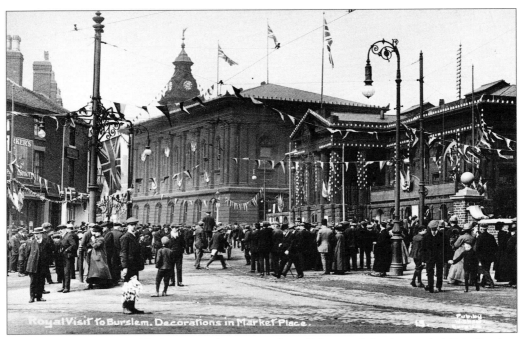

A good view of the 'Shambles' meat market, extremely well decorated for the royal visit to Burslem in 1924. Behind the market is the old Town Hall, suitably bedecked with bunting. As well as being a meat market the Shambles housed the locally famous 'Norris Wines & Spirit Merchants'.

With the old meat market gone Burslem waits with anticipation for the completion of the building that will house the 'Ceramica Exhibitions'. Items due to star in the exhibition were unearthed on the site during an archaeological dig by Channel 4's 'Time Team'.

CHAPTER FOUR
TUNSTALL

The clock tower, Market Square, Tunstall, 2000.

This photograph presents a view that is no longer available to us, the High Street, *c.* 1890. None of these buildings remains along this stretch of road.

Today's picture of the High Street is taken from a vantage point further up the road, to give a good indication of what it is like today.

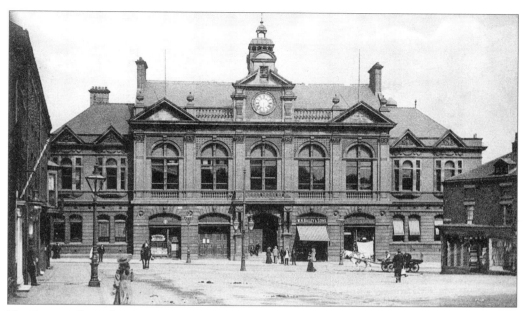

The Town Hall was built on High Street in 1885 at a cost of £14,000. Facing it is the clock tower (out of the picture), which stands on the site of the original Town Hall, built in 1816. This massive building faces Market Place and included W.H. Bailey & Son and the Criterion Restaurant.

Today the Town Hall is a sorry sight for the people of Tunstall; it has stood empty for many years and shortly after this picture was taken the building was surrounded by scaffolding. It seems that this building has an uncertain future.

The crowd has gathered around Tunstall Town Hall to hear a speech given by the mayor in honour of Queen Victoria's Diamond Jubilee, 1897.

If a speech were given today it is likely that we would watch it on the television; today it takes something special to draw a crowd. It has been a long time since the Town Hall has seen people 'en masse'.

Everyone loves a sale. Most residents of Tunstall seem to be in this shot outside Naylor's Bon Marché, within the Town Hall. Recovery from the war was a slow process and at the time of this picture, early 1950s, money was still scarce, which meant a sale of any sort was very welcome. The building to the right is the District Bank.

Along with the rest of the Town Hall this lies almost derelict. NatWest now occupies the District Bank.

A window display at Naylor's Bon Marché, showing the popular lines of the day.

Naylor's was a popular place to shop for the people of Tunstall, but it was later converted into a public house.

After eleven years in the making Victoria Park was opened in 1908; it boasted three bowling greens, a pavilion, a bandstand, fountain and tennis courts. This is a view of the Park Gates in 1913.

The scene here is little different today. The parks of The Potteries still attract a good number of people considering the number of competing attractions.

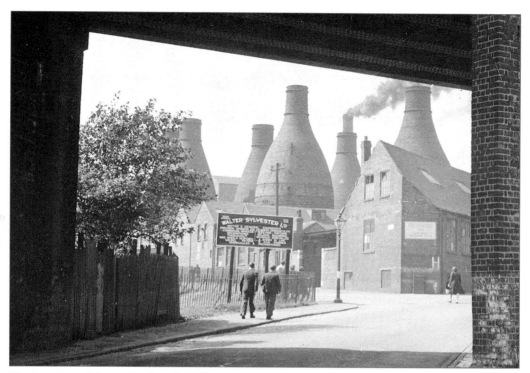

The junction of Scotia Road with Williamson Street from under the bridge, 1950. In the centre of the picture is a sign for Walter Sylvester Ltd, a general engineering firm of the time. Inevitably we see bottle ovens in the distance.

Williamson Street today has changed out of all recognition since the 1950s. Most of the buildings on either side of the road have been replaced and major development work is currently proceeding in this area; and of course the bridge has gone.

It would not have been difficult to identify where the post office was in Tunstall at the turn of the century. This ornate cast-iron sign hung above the door and was a pleasure to the eye.

The modern-day version does not boast the craftsmanship that singled out its predecessor, although it must be said it is still quite easy to find the post office.

Goldenhill stands to the north of Tunstall and is the home of the famous Goldenhill Wanderers football club. This is the High Street in about 1910.

Goldenhill Road goes into Kidsgrove, which comes under the Borough of Newcastle-under-Lyme. On the border can be found the Goldenhill municipal golf course.

Trubshaw Cross from Brownhills Road, with Arthur Wood & Sons' works, 1950s. Along with Middleport and Longport this area was industrial and residential, showing the unique co-existence of the two within Potteries towns.

The bottle ovens have gone, but this is one of the few remaining areas in the city where people and pots live together as they used to all over.

Scotia Bridge carried The Potteries loop line, which was part of the 'Knotty' (or North Staffordshire Railway), over Scotia Road. The Potteries loop was a line that linked the towns, and during the early part of the twentieth century it was widely used by the people of Stoke-on-Trent. With the rise of private transport the line became unprofitable, and it was forced to close in the early 1960s.

No longer of any use after the closure of the loop line, the bridge was eventually demolished. Although nothing remains of Scotia Bridge there is still a small section of a bridge at the top of Scotia Road, a little reminder of the 'Knotty'.

CHAPTER FIVE

FENTON

The Old Tollhouse was on the south side of King Street, and is seen here in October 1972. It was demolished in October 1974, the signs having been acquired by Stoke-on-Trent Museum in November 1972.

Victoria Place, *c.* 1915. Pottery manufacturer William Meath Baker erected the elaborate Victorian houses to the right of the picture in 1887. It is probable that the horse-drawn carts are carrying supplies to the Minerva potbank, which can be seen to the left. On the central reservation is a tram shelter provided by the Potteries Electric Traction Co. and a water fountain, which was later moved into the local park.

The Victorian houses have survived, but with the rapid increase in private transport the central reservation has been replaced by a roundabout. The Minerva works was demolished in the 1930s and this site has since been used for housing development.

Looking towards the south end of Manor Street, May 1977. At the end is the old Royal Oak, which had been built during the early nineteenth century, and to the left is the Fenton Working Men's Club and Institute. Although Fenton is the smallest of the six towns it still catered well for the drinking man of the late nineteenth and early twentieth centuries.

A modern structure now stands on the site of the old public house, but to the relief of the regulars it is still the Royal Oak. The Institute is now an Indian restaurant.

At the junction of High Street and Manor Street stands Elliot's Drapery in this picture of about 1905. As we can see, from all the extended canopies, the sun shone aplenty on Fenton this day. The row on the left is begun by the Royal Oak pub, whose landlord at this time was Tom Turpin.

The only buildings to remain today are sited at the junction, where Royal Oak Furnishings has been for many years. The Royal Oak has been replaced and all the buildings in the distance in the earlier photograph have been demolished.

Looking towards Stoke from City Road, May 1977. Central in this picture is the National Westminster bank and the old Royal Oak just before demolition in July 1977. In fact most of this scene was shortly to change.

Both the bank and the Royal Oak have been replaced by new buildings. In the distance we can see that a new development of multi-storey housing has replaced the row of shops that previously stood on the site.

The National Westminster bank on Christchurch Street is housed in the former Athenaeum. It was built in 1853, designed by Ward & Son in Italianate style, and became offices for the Fenton Board of Health in 1873. In 1889 it was adapted for use as a school of art by William Meath Baker, and was finally demolished in 1977.

The replacement for the former Athenaeum is not the architectural masterpiece its predecessor was; it is built in the then popular style of the 1970s.

Fenton Town Hall in Albert Square was built by William Meath Baker to the design of R. Scrivener & Son in 1888, and was occupied initially by the Fenton Board of Health and the Urban District Council as Baker's tenants. In 1897 the UDC purchased the building. It is a large red brick structure with stone dressings, designed in a mixture of Gothic and Tudor styles. Directly behind this building is Fenton Library, built in 1906.

In over 100 years the only development in this area is the landscaping of Albert Square and the addition of the war memorial; the building stands unchanged. It is now best known as Baker Street Court, although it does not actually front on to Baker Street.

Christchurch, May 1977. The church was built in 1890 on the south side of Albert Square and replaced the original 1839 structure; it seated up to 1,900 people and was designed by Charles Lynam. Its most striking feature, the tower, with a line of white bricks lying under the parapet, was added in 1899.

Christchurch is still in use today and remains one of the most original church designs in The Potteries.

Fenton Fire Brigade was established in 1859 when improvement commissioners purchased a fire engine. The offices for the brigade were next to the old market house. This is the fire station at Fountain Street in May 1977. It was built in 1909 and was in use until 1926 when the city's fire brigade was reorganised.

All the entrances fronting Fountain Street have been bricked up, and the old fire station now serves as offices for James Kent Ltd.

The old Salvation Army church in Fountain Street, May 1977. The church was built in 1912, and Mr W. Ball and Mrs M.C. Parkes, who were prominent supporters of the movement, laid foundation stones. The Salvation Army continued to use the building until it closed in 1972; it has since been home to Feature Designs.

Feature Designs left the building recently and it is currently being renovated. It is to become a mosque.

Until mid-1974 the junction between City Road (formerly High Street) and Wharf Street was the home of this array of unusual buildings, seen here in January 1973. Fenton, in keeping with the other towns, usually played host to the traditional terraced dwelling; however, these homes were of a much more individual design. This whole area was cleared to make way for the A500 D-road, which was to change the face of much of Stoke-on-Trent.

A roundabout now covers this site, which is totally unrecognisable as the one shown in the previous image. The A500 runs from junction 15 of the M6 motorway south to junction 16 north, cutting right through the heart of the city. This was a major project for Stoke in terms of transport and communication.

Here we see Temple Street Methodist chapel in May 1975. It was built in 1872 at a cost of £2,000. The foundation stones of the Chapel Hall, which stood alongside the chapel, were laid on 29 April 1973. The old chapel was demolished in 1975; after having fallen into disrepair its demolition was hastened by a massive storm, which left a large hole in the roof. The chapel was an excellent example of nineteenth-century Methodist architecture.

After the demolition of the chapel services continued in the chapel hall. A new chapel has now been built on this site; it was opened in the early 1980s.

CHAPTER SIX

LONGTON

Longton railway bridge, locally known as the viaduct, *c.* 1890.

Work was completed on Longton railway bridge in 1889; it carries the Stoke to Derby line. The most popular form of transport during this period, however, was the electric tram and in the centre of the picture passengers are waiting to board. This particular tram ran to Longton from Stoke. In the background stands the Crown and Anchor public house, dating from 1900, and also St John the Baptist's Church.

Although the railway bridge is still in use today this scene shows the transfer from public to private transport. The trams have long gone and the family car now reigns supreme. St John's Church has also left the scene, demolished in 1979, although the Crown and Anchor remains, now renamed the Crown Hotel.

This view shows Longton Town Hall in the 1930s, and it is apparent that the bus has taken over from the electric tram as the popular form of public transport (the last tram in the area ran in 1928). This building was the town's second hall and was built in 1863 from Hollington stone.

Although the main structure of the hall has been replaced the façade remains. In fact the only change obvious is the new road layout.

A closer look at the Town Hall, showing in detail the Italianate design, 1950s.

In 1986 a protest group saved this magnificent frontage from demolition.

This image dates from about 1910. In the centre a tramcar is making the slow climb up Stafford Street and on the left, on the corner of Heathcote Street, is the Wesleyan Methodist chapel. To the right of centre is one of the towers marking the entrance to the public market. This building was completed in 1863 as a dual project together with the new Town Hall.

Although the Wesleyan Methodist chapel was replaced by the Central Hall in the early 1930s the numerous other buildings running down the right-hand side of Stafford Street (renamed The Strand) have been retained. The Bennett's Shopping Precinct has replaced the shops to the left of the public market.

Longton, the home of the tram! Here we see a tramcar negotiating the incline of Market Street, 1899. Directly behind the tram is the Criterion Theatre and further down towards Market Place stood the Heathcote Arms and the offices of auctioneers E.J. Kent.

Little has changed in Market Street and many of the buildings seen in the previous image still remain, with only the first-floor frontage receiving a face-lift. It is notable, however, that many buildings are sadly lying unused.

The junction between Belgrave Road and Wise Street in Dresden, a suburb of Longton. Belgrave chapel stands majestically alongside the road of the same name. Along past the chapel runs a row of terraced housing reaching up to Cromartie Street and to the right is a row of shops, one advertising a public telephone.

The former chapel has now been converted into private apartments called Church Court. The terraced housing has been removed and in its place stands the Sutherland Centre, a healthcare unit connected to the local NHS Trust. The shops to the right are no longer with us, having been replaced by flats, and the area in the centre of the photograph is now landscaped.

A typical street scene in the suburbs of Longton at the turn of the century: terraced housing on either side of a narrow poorly maintained road. Cobden Street Methodist chapel stands on the right.

The terraces in Cobden Street have now all been replaced by modern housing and a new chapel complements the other buildings.

Trentham Road, *c.* 1900. On the corner of Belgrave Road stands the Lord John Russell public house (later replaced) with an old-fashioned gas lamp to accompany it. Notice the pony and trap just passing the pub; this was the only form of private transport available at this time.

Although the Lord John Russell is no longer with us, many of the buildings from the previous photograph still line Trentham Road, which is the main thoroughfare from Longton to Trentham.

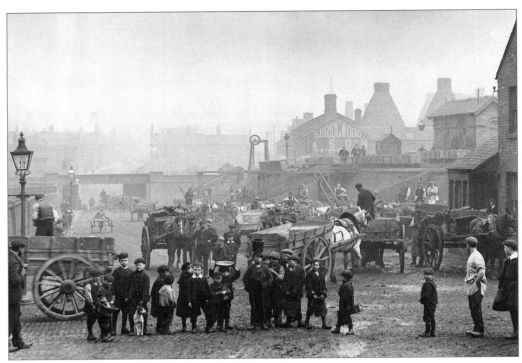

This image was caught by W.J. Blake in about 1904 and shows a group of children at Mansfield Colliery Wharf in Wharf Street, off Sutherland Road. During these hard times children would pick up the spillings from carts in the hope of either using or selling them.

Wharf Street has now been renamed as Bridgewood Street and this is the same scene about ninety-six years later. The children and the coal wharves do not feature any more, but it is still possible to place them here: imagination is a powerful thing.

An old potbank stands awaiting its fate, May 1975. During the 1970s many bottle kilns were demolished and the one we see here at Blue Bell Pottery, Barker Street (off Uttoxeter Road), was no exception.

From this picture it appears that the old potbank was demolished after it fell into disrepair. No development has taken place on this site in over twenty-five years.

The bottle ovens of Thomas Poole's Gladstone China works in Uttoxeter Road, 1971. The company ran until 1952, at which time the premises were occupied by Royal Stafford. This picture shows the site after production had ceased in the 1960s.

Gladstone Pottery Museum opened its doors on this site in 1975. It is a working museum and shows all the processes used in pottery manufacture over the last 200 years. The year 2000 marks the twenty-fifth anniversary of its opening. The photograph of the bottle ovens is taken from what is now the museum car park.

One of three almost identical buildings that graced Queens Park in the early 1900s. This fine structure in a half-timber design stood at the east entrance to the park.

This scene is almost unchanged in nearly 100 years, but the climbing foliage that once adorned the ground floor of the lodge is gone.

Four young children in the park, *c.* 1900. Although it was not unusual to see children in the park no provision was made for them. Opened in July 1888, Queens was the first public park in The Potteries and was sited on land given by the Duke of Sutherland. At the turn of the century it would cost the average potter a half day's pay to spend one hour upon the magnificent lake.

Although the children have gone Queens Park is still a popular place to walk, feed the ducks on the lake, or take in a game of bowls.

Pottery manufacturer T.C. Wild built the Alhambra Cinema in 1914 at Normacot, Longton. Thomas Clarke Wild was a councillor of Longton borough and in 1928 became the first Lord Mayor of Stoke-on-Trent. At the time of its construction the Alhambra was one of the first purpose-built cinemas in the area. The cinema closed in 1977, and in 1994 was demolished to make way for the new A50 dual carriageway.

At the time of demolition a protestor, Angie Stevenson, insisted that some part of the building be preserved. So strong was her insistence that the demolition team painstakingly numbered each brick from the façade; perhaps one day the Alhambra will rise again. The former location of the building is very different today; it is ironic that two no entry signs now stand where the entrance to the cinema once was.

A former chapel (dated 1889) in Edensor Road. This road ran through to the heart of Longton when this picture was taken in March 1975.

The building to the right of the chapel has been cleared away and is now a car park. Royal Essex Bone China now uses the chapel for storage and Edensor Road is now bisected by the new A50 dual carriageway.

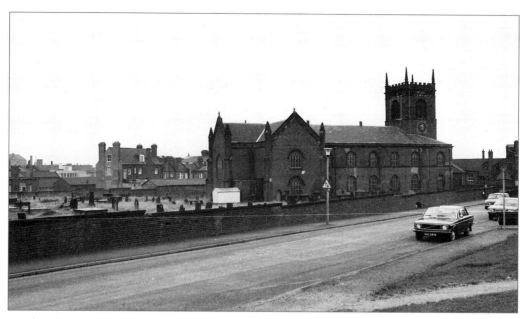

St John the Baptist's Church, February 1975. It was built in 1795 as part of Stoke parish; the church was a place of Anglican worship for 180 years. It was eventually demolished in 1979 because of mining subsidence. In the background stands the Crown Hotel.

The former site of St John's Church along Rutland Road can only be recognised by pinpointing the roof of the Crown Hotel standing in the distance. After demolition of the church the graveyard was cleared, and the site has been used for old folks' housing.

Longton Cottage Hospital was first established in Mount Pleasant in 1868 but, owing to the inadequacy of the accommodation, the Normacot building we see here was erected in 1890.

The 1890 building still stands, and Longton Cottage Hospital continues to serve the community some 110 years later.